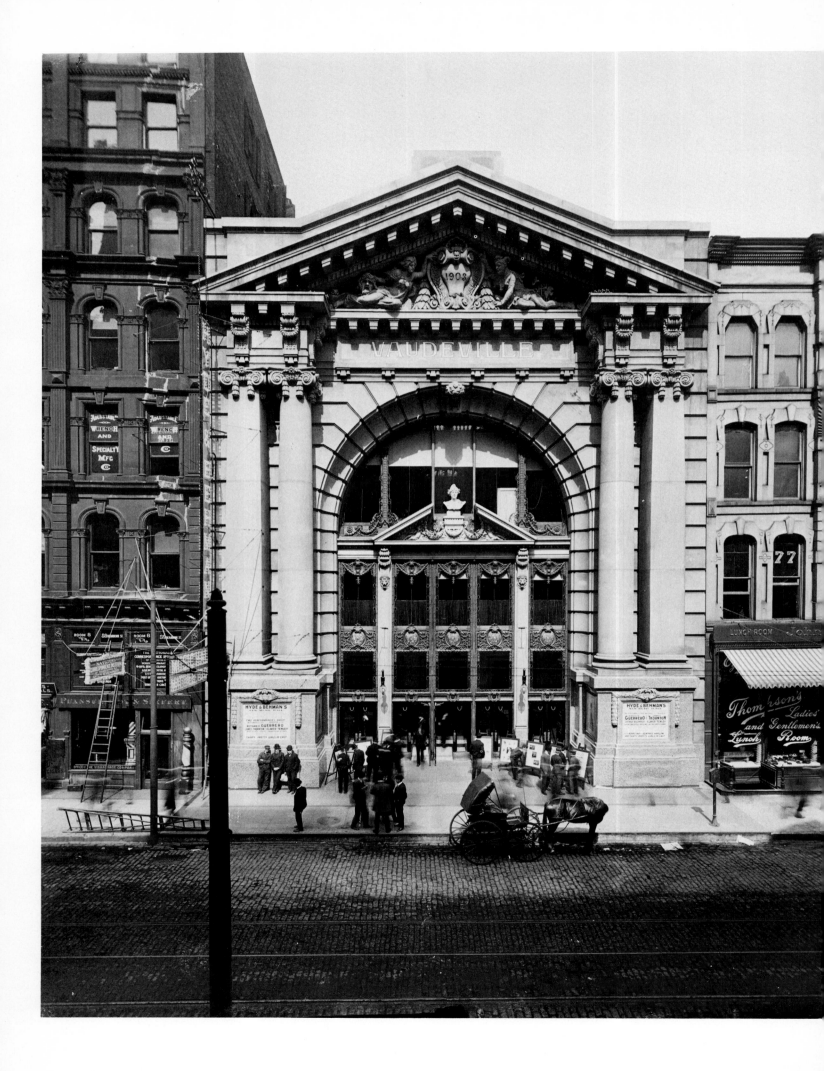

CHICAGO AT THE TURN OF THE CENTURY IN PHOTOGRAPHS

122 Historic Views from the Collections of the CHICAGO HISTORICAL SOCIETY

LARRY A. VISKOCHIL
Curator, Graphics Collection

with the assistance of
GRANT TALBOT DEAN
Associate Curator, Printed Collections

Chicago Historical Society

DOVER PUBLICATIONS, INC.
New York

Copyright © 1984 by the Chicago Historical Society.

Published in Canada by General Publishing Company, Ltd., 30 Lesmill Road, Don Mills, Toronto, Ontario.
Published in the United Kingdom by Constable and Company, Ltd., 10 Orange Street, London WC2H 7EG.

Chicago at the Turn of the Century in Photographs: 122 Historic Views from the Collections of the Chicago Historical Society is a new work, first published by Dover Publications, Inc., in 1984.

Manufactured in the United States of America
Dover Publications, Inc., 31 East 2nd Street, Mineola, N.Y. 11501

Library of Congress Cataloging in Publication Data
Main entry under title:

Chicago at the turn of the century in photographs.

1. Chicago (Ill.)—Description—1875-1950—Views—Exhibitions. 2. Chicago (Ill.)—Social life and customs—Pictorial works—Exhibitions. 3. Architecture—Illinois—Chicago—Pictorial works—Exhibitions. I. Viskochil, Larry. II. Chicago Historical Society.
F548.37.C52   1984   977.3′1104   83-20539
ISBN 0-486-24656-6

CONTENTS

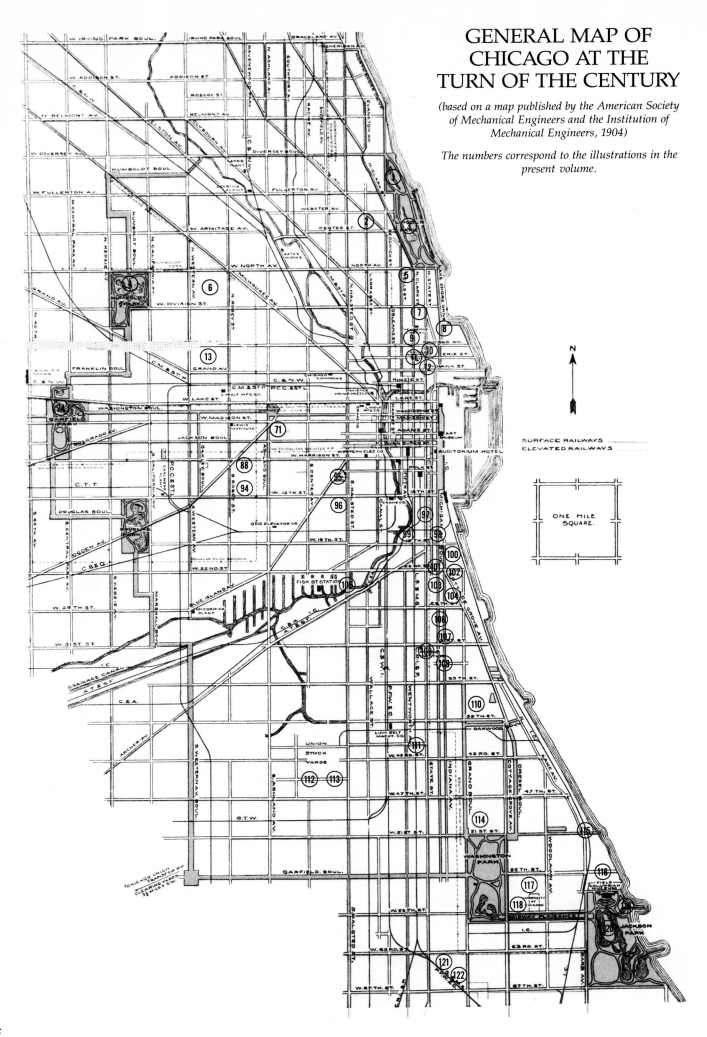

GENERAL MAP OF CHICAGO AT THE TURN OF THE CENTURY

(based on a map published by the American Society of Mechanical Engineers and the Institution of Mechanical Engineers, 1904)

The numbers correspond to the illustrations in the present volume.

SURFACE RAILWAYS
ELEVATED RAILWAYS

ONE MILE SQUARE.

THE CHICAGO LOOP (BUSINESS DISTRICT)
AT THE TURN OF THE CENTURY

(based on a map published by the American Society of Mechanical Engineers and the Institution of Mechanical Engineers, 1904)

The numbers correspond to the illustrations in the present volume.

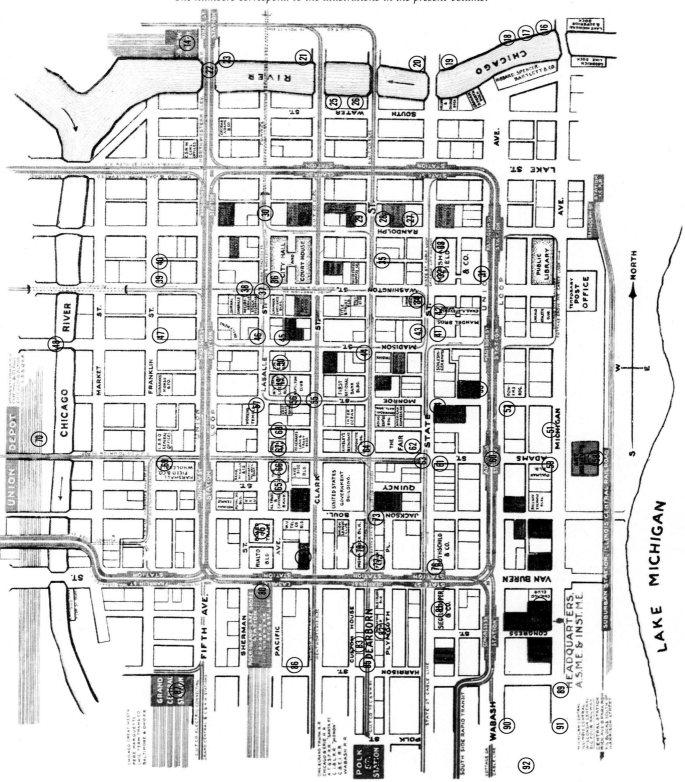

THE ELEPHANT THAT NEVER FORGETS

By the turn of the twentieth century almost anyone who could look at the evidence could see that Chicago was already America's second city. In less than a century it had grown from a small, remote military outpost and trading village to become the undisputed capital of the nation's heartland. Its position was all the more remarkable because only three decades before, in 1871, it had been almost leveled, flattened like the prairie from which it sprang, by what the whole world called the Great Chicago Fire. Few who had known the energy and enthusiasm of the city's entrepreneurs doubted the confident boast, "Chicago Will Rise Again"—bigger and better than before. Chicago's business community not only demanded the best but, more importantly, was willing to pay for it. The fire gave them, and the city's most imaginative engineers and architects, virtually a clean slate on which to plan for the reconstruction of a great urban metropolis.

By the end of the 1880s a new skyline was already taking impressive shape and the golden age of the Chicago School of Architecture had begun. In the next two decades most of the main elements of what we call modern architecture would be unveiled in Chicago for the world to admire and emulate.

The number of people drawn to this new city continued to grow at the impressive rate that had been characteristic of it from its beginnings. One year before the 1871 fire the population numbered 298,977. Ten years later it was 505,185 and by 1890 it was 1,099,850. Three out of every four Chicagoans were foreign-born or the children of foreign-born. By 1900 this immigrant population had swelled the total number of residents to 1,698,575.

Many more came to Chicago as tourists and visitors. The World's Columbian Exposition of 1893–94 attracted over 27 million visitors. Perhaps the biggest and best exhibit of the world's fair was the city itself. Even though the contrasts were great between the dream world of the White City and the reality of the grey and brown city surrounding it, in growth, opportunity and energy Chicago may have seemed to many a sightseer's eyes a city second to none.

The system of trolleys, trains, ships and carriages that transported visitors to and from the fairgrounds on the south side was part of an ever-growing network that spread from one of the most concentrated city centers in the nation. To feed this core of commerce, culture and services the latest methods of public transit were installed. The introduction of the cable-car trains in 1882 supplemented the horsecars. They, in turn, were replaced in 1906 by the electric trolley and the elevated steam railroad, both introduced in 1892. By 1897 the elevated train that "looped" the central business area was a reality. In a little more than a decade it, and other forms of public transportation, were bringing over a quarter of a million workers and shoppers each day to what, by then, was universally called "the Loop."

Many of these architectural and engineering marvels still exist in the 1980s and are used daily for the purposes for which they were built. To understand their use in the past and present, one has but to examine them. Additional insights into their importance to, and their influence on, the lives of the present and future residents of, and visitors to, Chicago can be acquired from historians and other commentators. Their written words are presumably based upon their examinations of historical evidence of all kinds. In actuality, most of the evidence that these commentators and interpreters have studied has been limited to textual sources. Perhaps many of their conclusions would differ had they devoted equal energies to the study of this city's visual records. This book, and the exhibition it accompanies, are an attempt to bring under closer public scrutiny some of Chicago's pictorial heritage and to examine the place photography may have in the study of the whys and wherefores of urban society.

The photographs reproduced in this book were selected from a collection of 300 glass, gelatin-emulsion, dry-plate negatives given to the Chicago Historical Society in 1938 by the Barnes-Crosby Company, one of Chicago's largest photoengraving firms at the turn of the century (founded 1897). Photographic contact prints made directly from these 11-by-14-inch plates provide a remarkable view of Chicago's built environment and a visual census of the city as it appeared during the early years of this century. They now comprise part of an archive of almost a million images that is the Graphics Collection of the Chicago Historical Society.

While individual items from the Barnes-Crosby collection have occasionally appeared in publications and exhibitions at the Chicago Historical Society since their acquisition, it was not until recently that all 300 were carefully cleaned and repaired by the Chicago Historical Society's photographic conservators, contact-printed by its photographers, identified and cataloged by its curators and made completely accessible for study and use by the general public. To celebrate the opening of the entire collection for research, and to make their availability more widely known, they are being formally exhibited in the galleries of the Chicago Historical Society in the spring and summer of 1984. The acquisition, display and publication of these images have been based upon one central assumption: that historical photographs should be considered both as vital tools for historical research and as aesthetic objects for pleasurable and informative viewing.

Almost from the moment when the daguerreotype process was revealed to an astonished world in 1839, arguments have arisen about what photography was good for. At first the users of this new medium were limited to those who had the time, money and talent to experiment with it—the very chemists, experts in optics and artists who had discovered and perfected the early processes. Later, as others began to grasp the implications of the discovery, each new explorer staked his claim to the products of the marvelous new machine for his own purposes. As the number of claimants to photography increased, philosophical arguments over the *proper* uses of photography were proposed and hotly debated.

Was photography a discovery best suited to serve as the handmaiden of art or of science? Was it chiefly for public enlightenment or for commercial exploitation? Would it function to preserve society's most significant past or only as an instrument envoking nostalgia and personal memories? Did it offer an opportunity to examine the world in a serious way or was it simply a clever toy? These questions, and others like them, persist unresolved to this day. The answers proposed remind one of the familiar English fable entitled *The Blind Men and the Elephant:**

It was six men of Indostan
  To learning much inclined,
Who went to see the Elephant
  (Though all of them were blind),
That each by observation
  Might satisfy his mind.

The First approached the Elephant,
  And happening to fall
Against his broad and sturdy side,
  At once began to bawl:
"God bless me! but the Elephant
  Is very like a wall!"

The Second, feeling of the tusk,
  Cried, "Ho! what have we here
So very round and smooth and sharp?
  To me 'tis mighty clear
This wonder of an Elephant
  Is very like a spear!"

The Third approached the animal,
  And happening to take
The squirming trunk within his hands,
  Thus boldly up and spake:
"I see," quoth he, "the Elephant
  Is very like a snake!"

The Fourth reached out an eager hand,
  And felt about the knee.
"What most this wondrous beast is like
  Is mighty plain," quoth he;
"'Tis clear enough the Elephant
  Is very like a tree!"

*Poem by John Godfrey Saxe (1816–1887), as reprinted in *The Home Book of Verse*, Vol. 1, ed. by Burton Egbert Stevenson, Henry Holt & Co., N.Y., 9th ed., ca. 1953.

The Fifth, who chanced to touch the ear,
  Said: "E'en the blindest man
Can tell what this resembles most;
  Deny the fact who can,
This marvel of an Elephant
  Is very like a fan!"

The Sixth no sooner had begun
  About the beast to grope,
Than, seizing on the swinging tail
  That fell within his scope,
"I see," quoth he, "the Elephant
  Is very like a rope!"

And so these men of Indostan
  Disputed loud and long,
Each in his own opinion
  Exceeding stiff and strong,
Though each was partly in the right,
  And all were in the wrong!

MORAL

So oft in theologic wars,
  The disputants, I ween,
Rail on in utter ignorance
  Of what each other mean,
And prate about an Elephant
  Not one of them has seen!

Though each of the disputants about the proper function of photography was also in the right, their "elephant" was also greater than the sum of its parts. With this moral in mind, how then should we determine the possible functions of individual photographs? To help keep the conclusions of our fable clearly before us, let us examine carefully one memorable image. Initially we know nothing about this photograph beyond what we can see by looking at it and by reading the title inscribed on it: "First Blind Massage Class in America/Peter J. Peel—Instructor."

This caption only partly answers the first question that is asked of every photograph (but not of every painting, drawing, etc.): What is this a photograph of? But while we have provided a title, there may be many other possible titles. The questions we ask of it may help us to expand and explain this image and to determine the ways in which it can be used. The methods we will apply to the analysis of this photograph can be used on the other photographs reproduced in this book and on millions of other historical photographs that are available for research.

To further understand what this is a picture of, what it means and what are its uses, we must try to determine the *circumstances* under which it was made, the *role* it was meant to play and something of the *intentions* of those who made it. Was it to be an aesthetic statement, a scientific record, an announcement of a newsworthy event, an attempt at public education, a call for reform, a business record, a visual training aid, a graduation picture, a public-relations handout or an organizational report? It could, of course, have been any, or even all, of these things. In fact, it could still play any of these roles, or other completely different roles, any one of which may be completely different from the original roles intended by the maker of this image. The answers, again, depend upon which part of the elephant one is touching. This opportunity for different interpretation becomes especially evident as we be-

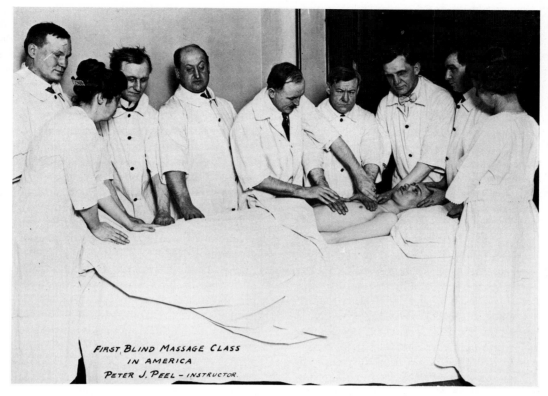

FIRST BLIND MASSAGE CLASS
IN AMERICA
PETER J. PEEL – INSTRUCTOR.

come aware how the different circumstances under which a photograph can be made affect how a picture looks and, consequently, what it means.

From the time of its invention, people have been attracted to photography because they believed that the camera could reproduce reality faithfully to the smallest detail. Because the vision of the camera's eye (so unlike our own) appeared so indiscriminate and unselective, the adage that "photographs don't lie" gained almost universal credibility. But later, as the proponents and opponents of various uses of photographs again looked at their "elephant" more closely, a new adage could be coined. It may be true that "photographs don't lie," but "liars do photograph." Photographic lies, like photographs, are not so much black and white as shades of gray. In order to detect which lies are little white ones, which lies are deep, dark deceptions, and which are not lies at all but simply less than the whole truth, the viewer of photographs must be prepared to examine carefully the circumstances under which the photograph was made.

To do this, the viewer must first get past the message (the subject matter of the photograph) and examine the message bearer (the photographic print) and the message sender (the photographer). This is no easy matter, for the objects depicted are very seductive, preventing the average viewer from going beyond his natural first question, "What is this a picture of?"

As important as "What?" are the other investigative questions—"Why?," "How?," "When?" and "Where?" These questions should be asked of photographs just as they are of any other sort of evidence that we study in order to reach a conclusion.

We have already questioned *why* our photograph of Peter Peel's massage class was made. We also need to consider *how* a photograph is made. If this information is not apparent on the print or from other written evidence associated with it, we need to examine the photograph closely and in detail. It is

often impossible to draw major conclusions on the basis of one image and, even if we were standing next to the photographer, we might never know all of the "hows" involved. We should be aware, however, that the photographer's technical considerations play a large part in deciding which truths (or "lies") we will see.

The equipment that the photographer selects will directly affect the kind of photograph he will take. If it is lightweight and small he may be able to take it to areas to which a large camera could only be moved with difficulty. The images that comprise this book were photographed with a large, heavy 11 × 14" view camera, no doubt accompanied by a heavy tripod and a case of 11 × 14" glass plates and holders. Where it was positioned greatly influenced the resulting images. Many photographs of tall buildings in this book were made with a camera with a wide-angle lens positioned on the upper stories of another tall building nearby. How different a photographic truth would we see if the photographer was differently positioned and if he was using another camera or a lens with a longer focal length? The length of the lens not only determines how much of the scene we will see, but how we will see it. A telephoto lens, for example, tends to compress objects that are in reality farther apart than they seem. How the lens is set and focused will determine which parts of the scene appear sharp or blurred. Even the optics of the lens can distort reality since images in the center of a lens are usually more distinct than those at the edges, where distortions are more likely to occur.

What the lens sees is indicated to the photographer by the camera's viewfinder. Through it the operator frames the scene, introducing further selectivity to the process. The lens indiscriminately takes in everything that the light strikes before it, differing markedly from human vision, which only focuses on one area at a time. Our eyes, however, are not restricted to what is within the final frame of the camera's viewfinder. This dual characteristic of every camera—that it seems to see too much and that it frames too little—must ever be kept in mind in our search for a truthful record. What is not contained within the frame and, consequently, not capable of being recorded in the photograph, is withheld from the viewer by the photographer. Is everything that we need to know about Peter Peel's class contained within the borders of our photograph? What might be missing? Were the camera lens and shutter fast enough to capture and hold movement, or was the scene posed? Was the film sensitive enough to record the correct color and tonal values of the scene? Were any real or imagined shortcomings of equipment or materials remedied by creative manipulations of the developing and printing processes in the darkroom? What subtle shades of meaning does the photographer impart to a photograph by his choice of developing and printing chemicals, photographic paper, filters, exposure times, cropping, masking?

Reality, of course, exists whether we see it or not. How a photograph was taken determines how much reality we can see. Therefore, if we can see the same reality in different ways, we can conclude that we are looking at *a* truth rather than *the* truth. The truth that we are given is the product of the imagination of the photographer, the mind of the viewer, the operation of the photographic equipment and materials, and the behavior of the subject in nature. Together they form a photograph that is greater than the sum of its parts and something that cannot be replicated exactly in the real world. The less each of these elements intrudes on, or intervenes in, the process, the more the result can be a truthful record of reality.

As we have just seen, there are plenty of opportunities for photographers to lie according to how each chooses to photograph what is seen through the viewfinder. The photographer can also falsify the scene itself by rearranging, adding and subtracting elements from it in such a way that he becomes a director rather than a recorder of reality. If his intentions are honorable ones, however, we can try to decide if his aims were primarily to interpret or to document the scene before him. Whether his motive is artistic expression, commercial marketability or scientific analysis, the reality he will photograph and present to us will depend largely on these intentions. Determining what these intentions were may be a difficult task.

Is it possible that the person who photographed Peter Peel and his students had heard of the fable of the Blind Men and the Elephant? If so, could he have purposely photographed the scene with the idea of symbolically and allegorically referring to the fable to make an artistic statement? It is possible, of course, but highly unlikely. By the end of the first decade after the invention of photography, most photographs were being made for commerce rather than for art or science. This trend has continued to the point where it is likely that almost every photograph that the average person sees today has been created for reasons other than the personal artistic expression of an individual photographer. While most photographs are not taken for art's sake, the intent need not be present for a photograph to succeed as a thing of beauty as well as a document of record. An aesthetic experience can as easily be produced by lucky accident as by intention. We wait until after our film is processed and printed to "see what we got."

Truth and beauty are not mutually exclusive but, if such is the photographer's desire, one can be sacrificed for the other. Objectivity may not be entirely attainable but it is a worthy pursuit. The artisan makes a detailed copy of reality while the artist creates his own reality—an original. To do this the artist may be willing to modify or subvert his results until they have little relation to reality. The artisan will attempt to show function while the artist is more interested in form.

The image that the artist creates may be a product of his imagination, reflecting his personality more than objective appearances. The art movements in vogue shortly before and after the turn of the century championed the subjectivity of the artist's personality over the objectivity of the camera. Peter H. Emerson, a noted fine-art photographer of the period, expressed this view: while "we cannot record too many facts in science, the fewer we record in art, and yet express the subject so that it cannot be better expressed, the better." Other photographic theorists went even further, claiming that photographs should look as much like paintings and as little like photographs as possible.

Most of them implied, in addition, that authorship was as important as intention. Anonymous works by anonymous photographers then, as now, seldom found a place in the published photographic histories or received serious criticism. These published histories relate the life, accomplishments and aesthetic intentions of known artists but offer little help in the subject analysis of their photographs. Art museums and connoisseurs who collected photographic works also cataloged and arranged their photographs by the name or school of the photographer, i.e. by their origin. It would be significantly different to categorize the photograph of Peter Peel and his class under such headings as "Physical Therapy" or "Manual Training Schools" or even "Allegory" rather than under the photographer's name if it was known. It is likely, of course, that it might not be collected by an art museum in the first place because of its anonymous creation.

Since "Anonymous" is the most prolific of all photographers, to exclude him from the world of art is to relegate him to the universes of science, commerce and amusement. There he will join the company of the millions of known and unknown photographers whose conscious intentions probably were to create something other than art. Despite the fact that these images are not the stuff of art histories, they make up the great bulk of the photographs available in the world's museums, archives and libraries. They have been collected primarily for their informational content and, though many of them are also beautiful objects regardless of their subjects, they have seldom been collected because of the artistic reputation of their creators. These cultural and commercial organizations collect "nonartistic" photographs because, for their purposes, the proper study of photographs can and should be more than art connoisseurship.

But knowing the photographer and his intentions does not, as we have indicated earlier, restrict the ways his images may be used and appreciated. Photographs created for the purposes of advertising, social reform, reportage and scientific exploration, and for many other commercial and personal reasons, have been appropriated by the publishers and purveyors of art even though artistic sentiments were secondary or nonexistent to their creators. It is clear that photographs need to be considered as both art and documentation. Whatever the photographer's intention, there is one requirement imposed by photography that sets him apart from the painter and the writer: the camera and/or its operator must be physically present when the image is made. It is in the role of witness that photographs gain their greatest credence as recorders of reality. Before photography, our view of important events and faraway places was as apt to be an artist's often whimsical notion of what things should look like as it was to be a literal description. If the artist had not been present on voyages of discovery, his view of the flora and fauna could include pictures of sea monsters as easily as of real elephant seals. By contrast, the photograph, almost by definition, is an automatic record—proof that something really existed.

The slice of time the photographer captures, the split second he releases his shutter, automatically transforms the present into the past. Another photograph of the same scene made only an instant later is different. Comparing the two, and other subsequent images of the same scene, offers a record of change that replaces our memory, allowing us to study it whenever we want. History is a mixture of science and literature and as such can no more offer an absolute record of reality than can photography. Like photography, it is a biased individual's interpretation of past reality. Photography can be the historian's natural ally, however, because it serves as a time machine in a way that no other communication medium can. In spite of the bias of its creator and interpreters, and in spite of the medium's visual selectivity, the photograph contains real data, available to anyone for any use. The information, emotions and perceptions present within the photograph are there for all to use. Since the photograph appears to be about its subject rather than about art, science or history, the average viewer feels that photography is an accessible medium, not something owned by the educated or the expert. Unlike writing, painting and other creative conceptual forms of expression, photography seems easily understood by anyone and everyone. The most unsophisticated viewer will willingly and confidently point out which photographs are "good" and which "bad." The "good" photographs are those closest to his vision of reality, those which closely mirror the world as he sees it. He lacks this confidence when confronted with paintings and other representations because the expert hand is more evident and intimidating. Everyone thinks he knows how a photograph should look. It is this comfortable feeling about photographs (enhanced even more by the apparent ease of using a camera) that makes photography the most democratic of arts.

This confidence grew throughout the short history of photography as technological advances rapidly placed cameras into the hands of an ever-expanding number of photographers. The difficult-to-produce, unique, positive-image daguerreotypes were soon supplanted by more useful practical formats that bonded wet collodion to glass plates to yield a negative from which unlimited paper prints could be made. These prints were cheap, convenient and widely available in various forms. They were most commonly distributed as cartes-de-visite, cabinet cards and stereographs. These card photographs were produced in the millions for sale to Americans of every economic class, who framed them in elaborately designed albums or placed them in special viewers for detailed examination.

By the 1880s and 1890s, only two generations after the widespread introduction of photography to the general public, two new innovations assured the medium's true universality: the gelatin dry-plate negative and the halftone method of photomechanical printing. For the wet-plate process to be accomplished, the photographer actually poured liquid collodion onto a piece of glass, placed the wet plate into his camera, made the exposure and then hurriedly removed the still-wet glass to a darkroom for immediate development. The introduction of the factory-cut and -coated, and much faster, gelatin dry plate freed the photographer from this burdensome and clumsy process, and allowed him to go anywhere more easily and quickly and take photographs spontaneously. The simplicity of dry-plate negatives and cameras made possible widespread amateur photography and greatly increased photographic activity and awareness in general.

The other great technical innovation was the commonplace distribution of photographs brought about by the development of photomechanical printing methods such as photogravure, the albertype process and, after 1890, the halftone process. Use of the halftone screen in printing gave an economical and practical means of approximating the continuous tones and details of a photograph. The ease of combining the halftone process with newly introduced high-speed printing presses made cheap publishing of photographs especially attractive. By the 1890s Chicago was clearly established as the center of printing and publishing in the West. With the capability of publishing photographs cheaply in books, magazines and newspapers the stream of photographic images before the general public became a flood. (This flood would swell to a tidal wave with the introduction by George Eastman and others of flexible roll film and of the Kodak and other cheap cameras truly usable by amateurs, and with the rise of the commercial photofinishing industry.) The results of these innovations may seem commonplace today but their impact on the spread of information and visual awareness shortly before and after the turn of the century was nothing short of revolutionary.

Between 1880 and 1890 the number of professional photographers in the United States increased from 10,000 to 20,000. From 1890 to 1900, it jumped again to 27,000. The great bulk of the photographs they produced, and the most common images that the average American was likely to see, were either studio portraits or scenic views. Portraits, of course, had been the staple of all photographers since shortly after the inception of photography and it continued to be so for both professionals and amateurs. For the most part, until the technical innovations just described became commonplace, photographing outdoor views of important buildings, public monuments, scenic wonders, great events and rural and urban landscapes had been limited to professional photographers or to amateurs wealthy and skilled enough to own the necessary complex apparatus. Architectural and natural wonders were photographed primarily because there was a commercial market for them. Many of the images produced by these commercial photographers survive because the architects, businesses, chambers of commerce and industry, railroads, tourist bureaus, publishers, printers and government agencies which commissioned them had a practical interest in protecting them.

While most commercial clients purchased large paper prints suitable for a variety of purposes, until the advent of photomechanical printing the average citizen saw many of his photographic landscapes and city views in the form of stereographs. The stereograph was composed of two small, nearly identical photographic prints mounted side by side on a card in such a way that, when viewed through a stereoscope, they would produce a three-dimensional image. From before the Civil War down almost to the outbreak of the Second World War, the stereoscope was as omnipresent in American parlors as television sets are today. Looking carefully at a stereograph collection of near and faraway places did as much to expand the average American's visual sophistication as it did his geographical universe. In many ways these little photographic cards prepared us for citizenships in the global village that later visual technologies would bring home.

Shortly before the turn of the century another important, but now often overlooked, visual document burst onto the scene: the picture postcard. It is thought that the photographs in this book were originally made to be used in the production of picture-postcard views of Chicago. Although such cards had been available in Europe earlier, postal regulations prevented printing a picture on a postcard in the United States until 1893. The first American picture postcards were issued that year in Chicago at the World's Columbian Exposition and soon became a national mania which reached its peak in the first two decades of the twentieth century. Their introduction coincided with, and partly resulted from, the technical innovations in photography and printing that were mentioned before.

The picture postcard represented the culmination of the growing demand for views that had characterized the entire history of photography. At the same time it was a natural extension of stereographic publishing. Photographic and lithographic views of faraway people and places, scenic wonders, historical ruins and impressive architecture fed the imagination of the armchair traveler and provided souvenirs for those few who personally made the Grand Tour of Europe, the Near and Far East and other exotic regions. While the exploration photographs of newly opened Western lands in America in some ways had served the same purposes (particularly as stereoviews), the picture postcard did so on a much larger scale. The subject matter of postcards, however, was usually less exotic fare. The primary subject of these cards, especially those produced by photographic means, was the American city and town.

Almost every main street and every object of civic pride in population centers of any size seemed to fall under the eye of the commercial photographers and postcard publishers. Photographers and publishers capitalized on the nationwide preoccupation with collecting souvenir views. The view cards they produced captured and promoted a sense of national identity in an era of great social change. Populations moved and shifted as wave upon wave of immigrants landed upon America's shores to join those who had preceded them to the nation's expanding urban centers and to the new small towns that sprang up across the continent. Coincidentally, new advances in engineering and architecture were almost daily adding awesome new structures to the skylines of Chicago and other cities, toward which citizens could point their fingers, and their cameras, with pride. The ubiquitous picture postcard's "wish you were here" message could, and did, promote people and places better than any Chamber of Commerce advertising copy.

For picture postcards to sell in the volume that would make it practical to produce them, they required popular subjects, a very low per-item production cost, a method of reproduction both cheap and attractive to mass tastes and an effective means of distribution. In most communities of any size, opportunity to supply this need was seized by a local businessman who set himself up as a postcard publisher. In small towns this publisher may have been any druggist or general-store proprietor, job printer, newspaper publisher or other entrepreneur who either produced the cards himself or acquired them from a larger publisher or printer and merely added his name to the cards. The photographs from which the picture postcards were copied were sometimes taken by the publisher or printer. More commonly, they were acquired from a free-lance commercial or amateur photographer who took the photographs on speculation or on assignment from the publisher.

The Barnes-Crosby Company, from which the Chicago Historical Society obtained these photographic negatives, was a prominent Chicago photoengraving, advertising-art and commercial-photography company. While the Barnes-Crosby Company may have also used these negatives for other purposes, it is likely that it either leased the rights to print these images to various postcard publishers or actually oversaw the printing itself. It is not known whether the anonymous photographer or photographers were employed by the Barnes-Crosby Company, if they were supplied by the postcard publisher or if they were free-lancers. In any event, some of the 11-by-14-inch glass negatives were printed and then reproduced photomechanically as colored 3½-by-5½-inch picture postcards by such well-known Chicago card publishers as the Curt Teich Company, the V. O. Hammon Postcard Company and the United Card and Novelty Company. Cards showing these views from these and other card publishers are found among the holdings of the Chicago Historical Society and, in large numbers, in the collections of every postcard hobbyist who collects Chicago views.

Although cards like these are valuable historical documents both for their subject matter and as artifacts of public sentiments of the period in which they were made, viewing them comes as a disappointment after seeing full-size prints from the original negatives. The postcards, in comparison, appear garishly colored, poorly printed, tiny—inadequate substitutes for the originals. They were often heavily retouched or even blatantly altered by publishers who added or subtracted elements that they felt might enhance sales. This practice underlines the necessity for those relying on pictorial records to, whenever possible, examine the original print or, even better yet, the original negative.

Examining what is shown in the photograph is, of course, only part of the story. The selectivity of the photographer and, by extension, of the commercial interests that hired him excludes more than it encompasses. Photographs of important architectural structures often isolate them from their urban context. Building interiors, and the activity that goes on there, are much less frequently disclosed than exteriors, both because of technical difficulties and because the market did not demand it. Of even less commercial appeal were scenes that exposed society's ills or, for that matter, even scenes that showed how and where the middle and lower classes lived. Even the photographs of such great pioneering social-reform photographers of the period as Jacob Riis or Lewis Hine were seen by very few members of the general public. Clearly, the photographer who took the photographs presented in this book had no mandate to expose anything unpleasant or to show anything detrimental to the reputation of the owners of the structures shown or the image of the sender or recipient of the postcards for which the photographs were made. This conscious, or more likely unconscious, censorship on the part of the photographer or his clients is partly inherent in the medium of photography itself. But the classical meaning of the word censor also applies to these photographs. In ancient Rome the job of the censor was to safeguard public morals *and* to take the public census. These and other visual records of the Chicago of 80 years ago are as capable of telling us about life at the turn of the century as any official census.

We must apply the same tests to these data that we would to any other primary source of evidence. To understand better what pictures are of, what they mean and what they can be used for, we must try to determine the circumstances under which they are made, the role they are meant to play and the intentions of those who made them. These photographs cry out for detailed analysis and interpretation by historians, geographers, sociologists, urban planners, engineers and architects, photographers, art historians and others who can find uses for them other than those for which they were originally intended. They serve as eyewitnesses with perfect recall of the past which, if we are careful to recognize their blind spots, will serve us well. And, whatever else we may ask of them, these "elephants" will never forget.

LARRY A. VISKOCHIL

IDENTIFYING THE PHOTOGRAPHS

Looking at photographs critically is often a demanding emotional, aesthetic and intellectual process. Our appreciation and understanding of a photographic image can be greatly enhanced if we know as much as possible about the objects recorded by the photographer. Descriptions of the subject content of photographs that appear in captions by the photographer or by the owner or users of the photograph can never be truly satisfactory because of the multiplicity of possible uses and interpretations. Nevertheless, some sort of initial identification is highly desirable if historical photographs are to be used efficiently.

When the Chicago Historical Society acquired, as a gift from the Barnes-Crosby Company, the 300 negatives from which the images in this book were printed, it did not receive any detailed accompanying written documentation. Aside from an occasional one- or two-word identification on the negative envelopes, all of the information that appears with the photographs in this book was arrived at through careful examination of the photographs themselves.

A detailed investigation with a magnifying glass revealed clues that helped to determine the date, location and subject of the photographs. Advertising signs, theater posters, street signs and building addresses, automobile models and license plates, clothing styles and other evidence were scrutinized and compared with other, already identified, photographs and with information found in printed sources, such as histories and directories. Knowledge of the history of some parts of the scene shown helped to date and identify other parts of the same image. Knowledge, for example, of the earliest or latest time a given form of public transportation could have been on Chicago's streets helped to date buildings shown in the same photograph. Most of the photographs in this collection appear to have been made in 1904 but some were made as late as 1913. Most of the photographs seem to have been taken from a southern vantage point so that when the sun was coming from over his shoulder the photographer would have been pointing his camera in a northerly direction.

The photographs are arranged in this book geographically from the north to the south side of Chicago and from east to west in tiers while moving south. A good working knowledge of Chicago's geography and architecture was essential in the identification process. I am grateful to Grant Talbot Dean, cataloger of books in the Chicago Historical Society's library for the last 30 years and one of Chicago's most knowledgeable experts on local history, for writing the captions in this book. The research necessary to identify the images for the captions was conducted by several past and present members of the Graphics Collection curatorial staff, by volunteers and interns, and by the historians and other researchers who have used these images since they were acquired 46 years ago.

L. A. V.

PRINTING THE BARNES-CROSBY NEGATIVES

There was a time when most photographers only made contact prints from their negatives. If you wanted an 11 × 14″ photograph, you made an 11 × 14″ negative. Though enlargers had existed as early as 1857, it is obvious that the Barnes-Crosby 11 × 14″ negatives were made to be contact-printed. One indication is that on many of these large glass plates the sky was masked out using a combination of heavy paper and an opaque solution. This masking produced a consistent white sky-tone and is especially noticeable around fine details atop buildings or along horizons where details like wires and poles tested the photographer's talent with the retouching brush.

The reasons for this "opaquing-out" the sky are several. First and foremost is the fact that until the 1920s black-and-white photographic emulsions were orthochromatic or "color-blind." "Ortho" emulsions render blue much brighter than red, producing black lips and white skies. Some photographers attempted to render a realistic sky-tone at times by using a horizon mask on the camera's lens to physically decrease sky exposure. Other photographers printed in clouds from specially exposed "cloud negatives." The public, however, seemed to be used to the "white sky" look and the "cloudy-bright" effect it lent to outdoor scenes.

Because of this sky masking, it may be said that the Barnes-Crosby photography represented a throwback to an earlier era when collodion negatives often yielded somewhat mottled, overexposed skies.

Another reason for opaquing the sky was the realities of contact printing. Unlike enlarging, in which the printer can locally manipulate exposure as the negative image is being projected onto the paper, there is no opportunity to "dodge" or "burn-in" when a contact print is made on a light box or printing box.

When these 11 × 14″ negatives were originally printed they were placed face down on a box that had a sheet of ground or frosted glass for its top side with a grid of light bulbs underneath. The printing paper (probably chlorobromide) was placed atop the negative, emulsion to emulsion, and held tightly in place by a locking, spring-loaded lid and exposed. Having the sky already masked out made it easier for the printer to concentrate on obtaining a good exposure for the subject matter.

Another sign that these negatives were made for the contact-printing box is the way some deep shadow areas are lightly masked. Though the printer could locally control exposure by varying the size of different bulbs in the light box as well as by inserting pieces of tissue paper between the ground glass and the bulbs themselves, neither method was as precise as the shadow mask.

Like the red and black "opaque" used to block out the sky, the shadow-masking solution was usually brushed on, though some more exacting applications required delicate airbrushing technique. This solution (one such formula being epsom salts mixed with stale beer) acted as a localized neutral-density filter and "opened up" shadow areas, making the images more suitable for reproduction. The somewhat haphazard masking visible on some of these negatives suggests that they were indeed produced for postcard use, where massive reduction would render any sloppy edges almost invisible.

Many negatives, especially the interior views, have such a tremendously long tonal scale that modern papers cannot fully reproduce them. Dubbed "bulletproof" by the old-timers, these extremely dense and contrasty negatives require a great deal of local control of both exposure and contrast to preserve detail in both the highlight and shadow areas.

In order for us to achieve the amount of local control necessary for reproduction, the Barnes-Crosby negatives were not printed with a light box but rather in a simple wooden contact frame using an Omega enlarger as a light source.

In addition to allowing the printer to control the intensity of the light source by adjusting the enlarger's lens opening, this method makes all matter of "dodging" and "burning-in" more practical and precise. Some negatives, however, are so dense that no picture detail is visible during what can be extremely long exposure times.

The paper used in printing these negatives was Kodak's variable-contrast Ektamatic SC. The speed and consistency of a machine-processed stabilization paper is a distinct advantage in projects involving hundreds of negatives. But even more important is the versatility of having a paper that allows the printer to vary the contrast within portions of a single image. Through the use of Kodak's Polycontrast, Dupont's (sadly discontinued) Varigam and several deep-yellow G filters (for extremely contrasty negatives), all the negatives were rendered printable. Some, like the interior view of the Rookery Building, required the use of three different contrast filters, high-contrast to pick up shadow details under the balcony, low-contrast to hold the skylight detail and a medium-low-contrast for the main body of the image.

Compared to much of today's 35mm photography, these virtually grainless 11 × 14″ contact prints have an astonishing wealth of detail. Close inspection reveals pictures within pictures, especially in the variety of turn-of-the-century street traffic.

Except for direct positive images like those achieved with Polaroid's new large-format color film (which is being credited for sparking renewed interest in large-format photography), contact prints of large negatives like the Barnes-Crosby 11 × 14″ examples in this book are as close as photographs on paper have ever come to the infinite detail of the finest daguerreotypes.

PAUL PETRAITIS
Photo Technician
September 1983

A NOTE ON THE CAPTIONS

The views are basically arranged geographically from north to south and, at each north-south level, from east to west (see the maps on pages vi and vii). The final element in each caption (in parentheses) is the Barnes-Crosby sequence number (in the form "BC-49"); these numbers are used in the exhibition and should be referred to whenever contacting the Chicago Historical Society for reproductions, further information, etc.

When the main subject of a photograph is a building (or a group of buildings), the caption includes the following information wherever applicable: chief name of building; alternate names (that is, earlier or later ownership, etc.) *in parentheses*; address; year of opening of building (these years are *not* the dates of the photographs); year of demolition, if known (in a range of dates, such as "1891–1936," the first year is that of the opening, the second year that of demolition); architect or architectural firm (without the word "architect"). Thus for example, caption 38,

Andrews Building (Herald Building), 161–65 West Washington Street, 1891–1936. Burnham & Root.

is to be interpreted as: "Andrews Building; also known as Herald Building; located at 161–65 West Washington Street; opened 1891; demolished 1936; designed by the architectural firm of Burnham & Root."

1. Lincoln Park Zoo. (BC-49)

3. Chicago Academy of Sciences, Clark Street at Armitage Avenue, 1893. Normand Smith Patton and Reynolds Fisher. (BC-62)

5. Germania Club, northwest corner Germania Place and North Clark Street, 1888. (BC-260)

9

7. Newberry Library, 60 West Walton Street, 1892. Henry Ives Cobb. (BC-99)

8. Water Tower and Pumping Station, looking southeast, 1869. W. W. ... Kinzie Apartment House on the southwest corner of Chicago and Michi...

9. Chicago-Clark Building (Bush & Gerts Building, Bush Temple of Music), northwest corner West Chicago Avenue and North Clark Street, 1901. John O.E. Pridmore. To the left is the Moody Church, then on the grounds of the present Moody Bible Institute. (BC-200)

10. Holy Name Cathedral, northeast corner North State and East Superior Streets, 1874/75. Patrick C. Keeley. (BC-192)

11. Chicago Historical Society, northwest corner North Dearborn and West Ontario Streets, 1896, vacated 1931. Henry Ives Cobb. (BC-139)

13. St. Mary's of Nazareth Hospital, 545 North Leavitt Street. (BC-237)

14. Chicago and Northwestern Railway Company station, North Wells and West Kinzie Streets, 1882–1927.

15. United States Life Saving Station, lakefront at mouth of river. (BC-178)

17.   The *Christopher Columbus* at dock at Rush Street. (BC-159)

48.   Pier crowds leaving port from Beach Street, Indianapolis ferry approaching. (PC 71)

19. The *Père Marquette* in tow at State Street; the Dearborn Street bridge is also open. (BC-146)

20. State Street bridge, one of the first swing-like lift or bascule bridges. (PC.)

21. Fireboats *Chicago* and *Illinois* just west of the Clark Street bridge. (BC-41)

23. Steamer *Alaska* at dock on east side of Wells Street. (BC-193)

25. South Water Street Market. (BC-201)

26. South Water Street Market. (BC-202)

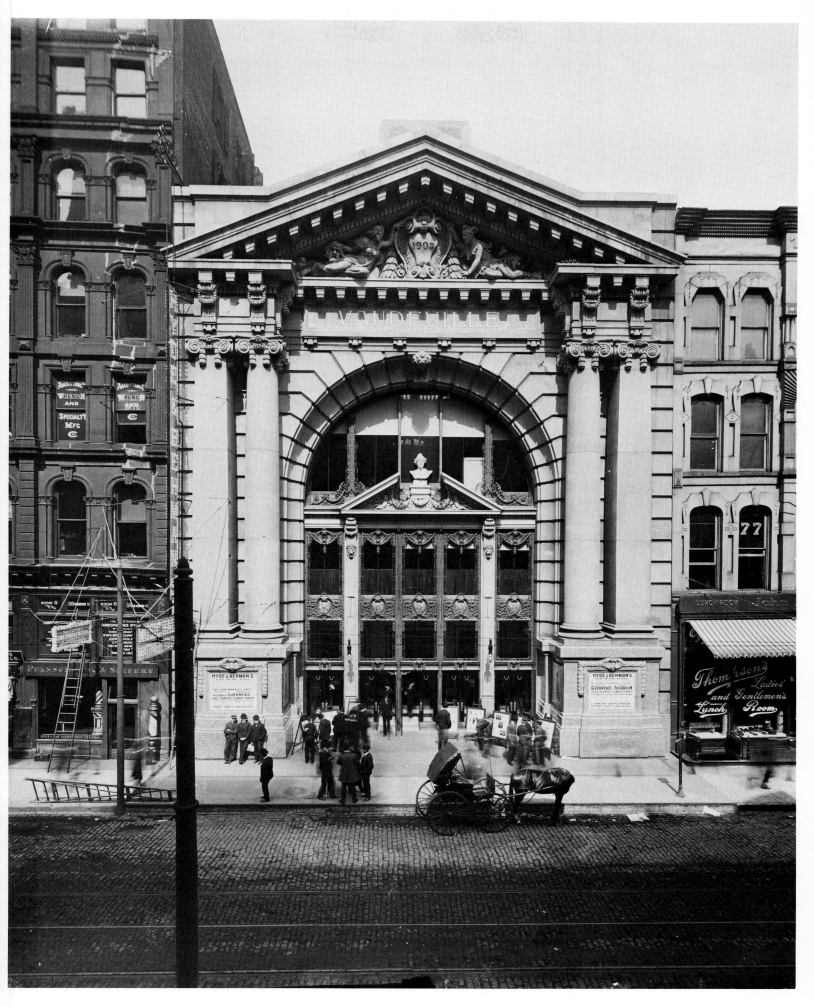

27. Hyde & Behman's New Music Hall (Iroquois Theatre, Colonial Theatre), a vaudeville house in 1904,
24–28 West Randolph Street, 1903–1925. Benjamin H. Marshall. (BC-138)

28. Northwest corner of West Randolph and North Dearborn Streets, Real Estate Board Building (Delaware Building), 1874. Wheelock & Thomas. (BC-262)

29.   Looking west on Randolph Street from Dearborn Street; the central building is the Garrick building and theater (Schiller), 1892–1961. Adler & Sullivan. (BC-15)

30. La Salle Street tunnel from Randolph Street. (BC-36)

31. John Crerar Library, located on sixth floor of Marshall Field & Co.'s building at corner of Wabash Avenue and Washington Street. (BC-144)

22. Marshall Field & Co., State Street, old front. Wabash and State, south reach by H.H. sometime about 1 1907

33. State Street entrance to Marshall Field & Co. (BC-165)

34.   Reliance Building, 32 North State Street, southwest corner West Washington Street. Four stories in 1890.
Burnham & Root. Ten stories added in 1895. D. H. Burnham & Co. (BC-252)

35.   Unity Building, 127 North Dearborn Street, 1892. Clinton J. Warren. Chemical Bank Building, 115–21
North Dearborn Street, 1898–1929. (BC-117)

37.   30 North La Salle Street, southwest corner Washington Street, Chicago Stock Exchange Building, 1894–1972. Adler & Sullivan. The entrance and the trading room are at The Art Institute of Chicago. (BC-8)

38.   Andrews Building (Herald Building), 161–65 West Washington Street, 1891–1936. Burnham & Root. (BC-58)

39. Interior of Engine House no. 40, 115 North Franklin Street. (BC-4)

41.   State Street north from Madison Street. (BC-294)

43. Champlain Building, northwest corner North State and West Madison Streets, 1894–1916. Holabird & Roche. (BC-240)

44. Hartford Building, 8 South Dearborn Street, southwest corner Madison Street, 1893, 1903–1968. East portion 1893, west portion 1903. Henry Ives Cobb. (BC-169)

45. Tacoma Building, northeast corner North La Salle and West Madison Streets, 1889–1929. Holabird & Roche. (BC-223)

46.   La Salle Hotel, northwest corner North La Salle and West Madison Streets, 1909–1976. Holabird & Roche. Note the photographer in lower right-hand corner. (BC-44)

47. Galbraith Building, northeast corner West Madison and North Frank-
lin Streets, 1873–1941. Contained the offices of Barnes-Crosby Company, the company that probably made or commissioned these photographs. Cochrane & Miller. (BC-203)

48. M. N.... S.... N.... M.... A..... B....

49. Looking north on La Salle Street from Arcade Place. (BC-47)

50.   Association Building (Central Y.M.C.A.), 19 South La Salle Street, 1893. Jenney & Mundie. Equitable Building, 29 South La Salle Street (National Life Building), 1902. Jenney & Mundie. (BC-102)

51.   Lake View Building (Municipal Court Building), 116 South Michigan Avenue, 1906. Jenney, Mundie &
Jensen. Illinois Athletic Club, 112 South Michigan Avenue, under construction, completed in 1908, now being
vacated by the club. Barnett, Haynes & Barnett of St. Louis. (BC-130)

53. Wabash Avenue, looking south from Monroe Street (RG3)

53.   Clifton House (Windsor-Clifton Hotel), northwest corner of South Wabash and East Monroe Streets, on site of present Carson, Pirie, Scott & Company store, 1873–1927. John M. Van Osdel. The Church Building, 1903, now occupied by Carson's. Hill & Woltersdorf. The J. P. Atwater Building is also occupied by Carson's. (BC-19)

54. Palmer House (number three), southeast corner East Monroe and South State Streets, 1875–1923/25. John

55.   105 West Monroe Street Building (Standard Trust & Savings Bank, Fort Dearborn Building), southwest corner South Clark and West Monroe Streets, 1895. Jenney & Mundie. (BC-249)

56.   Another view of 105 West Monroe Street Building with the four floors and a bay added on the south end in 1905. Jenney & Mundie. (BC-128)

57.   Women's Temple, 102–16 South La Salle Street, southwest corner of West Monroe Street, 1892–1926.
Burnham & Root. (BC-133)

58. Art Institute of Chicago, South Michigan Avenue at Adams Street, 1892. Shepley, Rutan & Coolidge. (RC 219).

59.   Pullman Building, 79 East Adams, southwest corner South Michigan Avenue, 1884–1956. S. S. Beman. Notice the Orchestra Hall building just being started in 1904. (BC-111)

60. Wabash Avenue looking north from Adams Street elevated station. (BC-157)

61.   Republic Building, 209 South State Street, southeast corner East Adams Street, 1905–1960. Holabird & Roche. (BC-78)

62. Fair Store, on north side of West Adams Street between State and Dearborn Streets, 1892. Jenney &

63. West side of State Street looking north from Adams Street. (BC-57)

64.   Marquette Building, 140 South Dearborn Street, northwest corner of West Adams Street, 1895. Holabird & Roche. (BC-52)

65. Rookery Building, 209 South La Salle Street (east side) between Adams and Quincy Streets, 1886. Burnham & Root. (BC-186)

67.   Home Insurance Building, northeast corner South La Salle and West Adams Streets, 1885–1931. William Le Baron Jenney. (BC-291)

69. Marshall Field & Co. Wholesale House, bounded by Adams, Franklin, Quincy and Wells Streets, 1887–1920. Henry Hobson Richardson. (BC-131)

70. Pennsylvania Limited arriving at Union Station, the viaduct of the West Side Elevated Railway at Adams

71. Church of the Epiphany, southeast corner Ashland Boulevard and Adams Street, 1885. Edward J. Burling and Francis Whitehouse. (BC-244)

72. Stratford Hotel (Gardner House, Leland House), southwest corner of South Michigan Avenue and East

73. View of South Dearborn Street from Fisher Building: Monadnock,
Federal Building (1905–1965, Henry Ives Cobb), Marquette on the left; Great
Northern Hotel (1892–1940, Burnham & Root); Great Northern Office and
Theatre Building (1895–1960, Daniel H. Burnham) on the right. (BC-257)

75.   Board of Trade (number three), 1885–1929, 141 West Jackson Street; a 300-foot tower was removed about 1895. W. W. Boyington. (BC-285)

77.   Fisher Building, 343 South Dearborn Street, northeast corner Van Buren Street, 1896. D. H. Burnham.
The building was enlarged on the north in 1907. (BC-175)

78.   Monadnock, on block bounded by South Dearborn, West Jackson, South Federal and West Van Buren Streets. View from the south. North half originally called Monadnock and Kearsarge Buildings (highest and heaviest wall-bearing building in Chicago), 1891. Burnham & Root. South half originally called Katahdin and Wachusett Buildings, 1893. Holabird & Roche. (BC-191)

79. Victoria Hotel, 330–38 South Clark Street, northwest corner Van Buren Street, 1885. Gregory Vigeant. (BC-280)

81. Siegel, Cooper & Co. (Leiter Stores; Sears, Roebuck & Co.), east side of South State Street between East Congress and East Van Buren Streets, 1891. Jenney & Mundie. (BC-297)

82. Dearborn Street looking north from Congress Street; from right to left, Como (1887–1938, John M. Van Osdel), Manhattan (1890, W. L. Jenney), Plymouth (1899, Simeon B. Eisendrath), Old Colony (1894, Holabird & Roche) and Fisher Buildings. (BC-298)

83.   On the left, Caxton Building, 500–08 South Dearborn Street, 1890–1947. Holabird & Roche. On the right, Monon Building, 436–44 South Dearborn Street, 1890–1947. John M. Van Osdel. (BC-55)

84.   Fine Arts Building (Studebaker), 410 South Michigan Avenue, 1886. S. S. Beman. (BC-287)

85.   Pontiac Building, northwest corner South Dearborn and West Harrison Streets, 1891. Holabird & Roche. (BC-195)

87.   Grand Central Station, southwest corner Wells and Harrison Streets, 1890–1969. S. S. Beman. (BC-85)

88. Cook County Hospital, West Harrison and South Wood Streets, 1882. John Crombie Cochrane, architect;
George Messersmith, sculptor (Photo: Lee Lawrie collection, ICHi-12610).

89. Michigan Avenue north from Auditorium Annex (1893, Clinton J. Warren, later Congress Hotel) and Auditorium Hotel (1889, Adler & Sullivan, later Roosevelt University) to the Montgomery Ward Building (with tower, in background). The Art Institute is to the right. (BC-143)

90.   Brunswick Building, 629 South Wabash Avenue (Studebaker Building), 1895. S. S. Beman. (BC-179)

91. Michigan Avenue from Balbo Street north to Van Buren Street. Black-
stone Hotel (1909, Marshall & Fox), Musical College Building (1908, C. A.
Eckstorm, later Blum Building), Dennehy Building (1913, Zimmerman,
Saxe & MacBride, later Petroleum Building), Harvester Building (1907,

C. A. Eckstorm, later Fairbanks-Morse Building), Congress Annex Hotel
(1902, Holabird & Roche, later "Annex" was dropped), Auditorium Annex,
Auditorium Hotel, Fine Arts Building, 318 South Michigan Avenue Building. (BC-153)

93. Dearborn Street (also called Polk Street) Station, Polk Street at the foot of South Dearborn Street, 1883. Cyrus L. W. Eidlitz. (BC-101)

94. National League (Cubs) West Side Ball Park, West Polk Street between Lincoln Street (now Wolcott

95. Hull House complex, 800 South Halsted Street. The house and dining hall are still standing, but neither is visible in this view. Now the campus of University of Illinois at Chicago. (BC-288)

96 Maxwell Street (RC 155)

97. Coliseum, Wabash Avenue at 15th Street, 1899–1983. Two small portions of the stone wall still remain on the site. (BC-227)

99.   The *Arthur Orr* at Armour Elevator E on south branch near 16th Street.   (BC-120).

100. Fort Dearborn Massacre Monument, 18th Street and Calumet Avenue, east of George M. Pullman residence. Now in storage. Model of *____* Chicago Historical Society. Original base has been destroyed. Dedicated

101. Calumet Club, South Michigan Avenue, northeast corner 20th Street (now Cullerton). (BC-196)

102.   Sinai Congregation, Indiana Avenue, southwest corner 21st Street, 1876–1912. (BC-296)

103. Lexington Hotel, northeast corner Michigan Avenue and 22nd Street. (BC-34)

104.   Metropole Hotel, South Michigan Avenue at 23rd Street. (BC-274)

105.   Halsted Street vertical life bridge on the south branch. (BC-160)

106.   Michigan Avenue looking north from below 26th Street. Trinity Episcopal Church, on the southeast

107.   Potomac Apartments, southwest corner Michigan Avenue and 30th Street. (BC-198)

108. Armour Institute (now Main Building, Illinois Institute of Technology). [. . .] Exterior. [. . .]

109. 3358 South Michigan Avenue on corner, 3344 and 3340 to the right. (BC-217)

110.   Wendell Phillips High School, 244 East Pershing Road, 1904. William Bryce Mundie. (BC-126)

111. Pennsylvania Limited between Englewood Station at 63rd Street and downtown. (BC-234)

113. Union Stock Yards, Exchange Avenue at Peoria Street, 1879. Burnham & Root. The only remnant left of the Yards. (BC-107)

115. Chicago Beach Hotel, Hyde Park Boulevard at the lakefront, 1893–1926. (BC-293)

116. Windermere Hotel,

117. Hull Court, University of Chicago, looking northwest; left, Culver Hall; right, Anatomy Building, 1897. Henry Ives Cobb. Hull Court and gate by Olmsted Brothers, 1903. (BC-71)

118. Hutchinson Hall, University of Chicago, Mitchell Tower, Reynolds Club, Leon Mandel Assembly Hall

119. German Building in Jackson Park from the lakeshore, 1893 (built for World's Columbian Exposition). Johannes Radke. (BC-24)

121. White City in its first season, 1905, looking south from the entrance on 63rd Street. (BC-123)

INDEX

The numbers are those of the illustrations.